SHAME

EXPOSING THIS CORROSIVE ENEMY

PETER WILKS

RED BALLOON
PUBLISHING

COPYRIGHT

Copyright © 2020 by Peter Wilks

All rights reserved.

No part of this book may be reproduced in any form or by any electronic or mechanical means, including information storage and retrieval systems, without written permission from the author, except for the use of brief quotations in a book review.

Scripture quotations are taken from the New American Standard Bible® (NASB), Copyright © 1960, 1962, 1963, 1968, 1971, 1972, 1973, 1975, 1977, 1995 by The Lockman Foundation Used by permission. www.Lockman.org

DEDICATION

I dedicate this book to my friend, Pastor Eder Goncalves, the only Brazilian Senior Pastor (currently) in Scotland. He encouraged me to teach a 6-week class with him, called *The Clinic of the Mind* at his church, Leith Baptist. In preparation I produced a rudimentary teaching on SHAME. This proved a valuable source of understanding and 'revelation' for some of the folk who attended the course. I have updated and added to it since then. Thank you Eder for your ongoing friendship and encouragement.

ABOUT THE AUTHOR

Peter Wilks is a graduate of the *London School of Theology* and a former Chief Officer of *MV Logos*, the mission ship that sails the globe taking the gospel to the nations, run by the charity *Operation Mobilisation*. Since then Peter has taught with Rev. Rod Anderson at *Liberty Bible Training Centre*, and has assisted Rod and Julie Anderson in the formation and ongoing growth of the international prayer ministry, *Prayer for the Nations*. More recently he was included on the Bible teaching staff of *Christ for the Nations UK* and has been involved in pastoral ministry.

Peter also accepted the position of Global Communications Co-ordinator for *Go to The Nations* (GTTN). In this capacity he regularly travelled abroad with GTTN teams to support churches in Europe and further afield, seeking to encourage and raise up the next generation of the church.

Peter retired from a position on the leadership team of *Shore Community Church* (formerly Open Gate Church) in Bognor Regis UK, in 2016. Since then he has continued his support for the GTTN vision by engaging with *Open Heart Church* in Bognor Regis and Portugal. He has a strong desire to see people grow in their intimacy with Jesus. This is expressed in the books he has authored. Peter recently became a director of *Red Balloon Publishing*. Peter and his wife, Felicity, have three adult children.

Further resources by Peter, and contact details, can be found at:

www.1thing.life

www.redballoonpublishing.co.uk

ACKNOWLEDGMENTS

A huge thank you to my wife, Felicity, who has borne the brunt of my writing 'tunnel vision.' She has, frustratingly for her, learned not to ask things like 'Shall we do a dump run this morning?' when I am deeply hunched over my computer keyboard!

I love you so much.

CONTENTS

EPIGRAPH

The difference between guilt and shame is very clear—
in theory. We feel guilty for what we do. We feel shame
for who we are.
Lewis B. Smedes

Live in thy shame, but die not shame with thee!
William Shakespeare: Richard III

Shame is like everything else; live with it for long
enough and it becomes part of the furniture.
Salman Rushdie

INTRODUCTION

Because of mankind's innate need to experience being valued, worth, love and belonging—it is easy to understand why shame is often described as the 'master emotion.' It is certain to destroy the wholesome experience of worthiness.

This book uncovers shame, and exposes it for what it is. It may be an uncomfortable read for many. Indeed, the most potent force shame can wield is the power of denial, 'No, that is not me! I don't suffer from shame.'

Shame hates being uncovered—even a little bit. Shame has embedded itself right in the heart of the human soul and steadfastly refuses to budge.

Shame is a corrosive force. However, there is good news! We can recognise it by what it says. Shame says: '

'I am un-lovable; I am no good; I am not good enough; I am not worthy; I am too fat; I am too thin; I hate myself; nobody likes me,' etc.

Shame encases the human soul and keeps it in a dark place, isolated and alone—the very opposite to how we were originally designed.

If you recognise you are under the thumb of this ogre, then 'shame management' is a way of controlling its sway over you. Many people, who we may believe have a good self image, probably manage the shame issue without realising it. But management doesn't eradicate.

Finding a measure of love and belonging in different types of relationships will curtail shame, but shame will still lurk beneath the surface taking any opportunity to rear its ugly head, especially when personal accusations are made.

But we need to go deeper to find the real answer. When we do, we find there IS a way to completely eradicate this unwanted spectre. That is, to DIE to it.

So, how does that work?

This little book helps us examine the options—shame management vs. dying to shame—becoming a corpse, and denying 'shame' any control over you anymore and <u>finally</u>, what that really means.

SHAME: ENEMY OF WHOLEHEARTED LIVING

Can you imagine the effect on an actor, of being thrust onto the stage in front of a huge audience, dazzled by the footlights, neither knowing his lines nor the character he or she is meant to be portraying? That would be the actor's worst possible nightmare!

The second worst nightmare would be, having learnt their lines, run through many rehearsals, then on the first night in front of an audience, suffering from stage fright and falling apart.

Imagine that was you—thrust out on to the open stage, exposed, with an auditorium awaiting your performance, and you had no idea what to do next. You would desperately want the floorboards to open and swallow you up or the lights to go out. Either way, a sudden departure into darkness and obscurity would probably be your fervent desire.

This might be a rather extreme example to highlight an issue we all struggle with—namely our performance of what is expected of us in everyday life, in different situations and circumstances.

We are all called to perform but it is the expectation behind that performance which is the crucial factor; the fluid scale determined not by any external criteria but by the fickle barometer of our own feelings in relation to how others will perceive us—according to our performance, including the way we look.

The result of dramatically failing to perform on the stage will initiate a cycle of feelings, beginning with a growing sense of embarrassment. The fact that we are alone and exposed induces a sense of guilt, that 'I have done something wrong', which very quickly turns into an intense rising tide of shame—which screams: 'I am wrong, I am a failure'.

Gershen Kaufman (a Professor in counselling) said, 'Shame is the most disturbing experience individuals ever have about themselves; no other emotion feels more deeply disturbing because in the moment of shame the self feels wounded from within'[1].

However, let's begin by considering anxiety.

2

ANXIETY

Anxiety includes a range of emotions, and the majority of them are triggered by us becoming the focus of other people's attention in some way or another. This is not to negate anxiety we feel over sickness, travelling, danger, decision making etc. Nevertheless the need for recognition, attention, to be approved and valued is the consistent factor in our humanity upon which anxiety feeds.

The anticipation of others' opinions of us can make us anxious if they reinforce <u>negative beliefs we already hold about ourselves</u>. This anxiety always has a negative effect. This generates feelings of fear.

Within this context there are four main areas that can cause us anxiety, with different degrees of intensity:

1. **Embarrassment.** This is the least serious of the four. It is normally fleeting and it can eventually be funny. Nevertheless, this emotion is activated when I feel I look *foolish* in other people's eyes. Therefore, anxiety arises when I am encountering a situation where I am unsure of the social codes or am a stranger among others. I do not want to draw attention to myself or be exposed.

2. **Humiliation.** Humiliation is the way in which you feel you're perceived a *failure* by another person. You can be made to feel humiliation by some inability to produce a good piece of work —as far as the other person is concerned. Humiliation is especially uncomfortable if your failure is exposed to those people around you. Listen to your self-talk. If your self-talk is 'My boss has gone over the top, it's not my fault, I don't deserve this,' that's humiliation. You can get over it. Anxiety is triggered when we believe we may be exposing ourselves to humiliation.

3. **Guilt.** Guilt is best expressed as knowing or believing *I have done something bad*. Guilt is what we experience when the action or deed breaks certain social codes, or the law. Guilt says I deserve punishment. It is the anticipation of being found out or having to confess our

fault and experiencing punishment which causes a high level of anxiety.

4. **Shame.** Shame is founded in *what you believe about yourself*, when you feel you 'are bad' in and of yourself. It is fundamentally negative.

So far then...

Anxiety is the common factor that we feel when we are potentially facing situations where we may be exposed and judged a lesser being by others.

We can and do get over embarrassment, humiliation and guilt.

Embarrassment is often momentary.
Humiliation can be overcome.
Guilt can be forgiven.
However, shame says:
'I am not enough; I can never be enough; I shall never be included, loved or find peace and belonging.'

What we believe about ourselves is a fundamental source of our anxiety.

Few of us can even dare take the risk of looking at ourselves, because the depressive nature of such thoughts is too strong. It takes courage to examine our own hearts. So then, how do we manage to overcome anxiety on a daily basis?

We blame others for what we are feeling. We say:

'It's her fault.'

'It's his fault.'

'You don't love me enough...'

The list is endless. What we do is find a scapegoat for our anxiety.

In being able to blame someone else for what we are feeling, we experience a release from our anxiety. But it only brings a temporary sense of peace. Therefore we are always looking to scapegoat someone. The scapegoat suffers our 'violence' to the degree to which anger has built up within us about the way we feel about ourselves, because we hate feeling this way. We somehow should believe better about ourselves but we are trapped and cannot find a way out. We can easily think even God hates us!

Shame is the source of our negative emotions. Shame lurks just below the surface of these felt emotions, whether anxiety, embarrassment, humiliation or guilt. Shame will often manifest as anger, which we will then vent upon someone else, blaming them for the way we feel. Domestic relationships are often the most vulnerable to finding such an easily accessible scapegoat.

Self-Talk

How we talk to ourselves about what is happening within us can reveal a lot about how we think of ourselves.

For example, let's say you forgot that you made plans to meet a friend at midday. At 12.15, your friend calls and asks if you are okay? If, at this point your self-talk is 'I am such an idiot, I'm a terrible friend and a total loser,' that is <u>Shame</u> talking! If, on the other hand your self-talk is, 'I am so sorry I forgot. What a terrible thing to do!', that is <u>Guilt</u> talking and it can be forgiven.

Guilt can be forgiven and released. Shame cannot. Shame is what you believe about yourself. Guilt is an aspect of shame but its influence can be positive because I can choose to change my behaviour(s) that caused the guilt.

Receiving forgiveness from others or from God for our guilt is one thing. But it does nothing to deal with the source of guilt—shame.

We believe God forgives our sin when we do wrong for which we feel guilt, and our guilt is forgiven. We go to others whom we have wronged, and some go to church to ask for forgiveness from God for the guilt we feel. However, receiving forgiveness from others or from God is one thing, but it does <u>nothing</u> to deal with the source of guilt, which is shame.

Many Christians find themselves stuck in the cycle of the forgiveness of sin and guilt stage, but never become vulnerable before God, thereby allowing Him deal with shame. It is simply too painful, so we continue dealing with shame in the only way we know that works—namely, the scapegoat mechanism.

❧ 3 ☙

PERFORMANCE SHAME

Performance shame is the belief that 'I am acceptable to the degree to which I am successful in life, work, and/or home.'

Shame is that terrible, private feeling that something is wrong with us—that we are somehow defective as a person. That we are irreparably damaged.

The voice of shame niggles away repeating, 'I am not good enough' or 'I will never amount to anything,' and the belief about myself that I would be rejected if anyone really knew what I was like.

Shame Loves Conditions

In defence of such negative thoughts we turn to doing something about it, and offer as answers a list of conditions to be met. Most of these conditions fall in the categories of performance, accomplishments, acquisitions and external acceptance I'll be worthy when... 'I will be good enough if...' They may not be written down, and we may not be aware of such conditions, but we all have a list that says I'll be worthy.......

When I lose weight
If I get accepted in this school
If I get promoted
If my marriage is successful
When I am good enough
When I achieve ....
When I'm attractive enough
When I'm important, etc.

Worthiness, however, requires no conditions

Perfectionism provides another list of conditions, which teach us to value what other people think about us rather than what we think or feel, or more importantly knowing where our real value is found.

Perfectionism defends shame. It is the belief that if I do things perfectly and look perfect, I can minimise the pain of blame, judgment and shame. Shame is painful because it is inextricably linked to the fear of being unlovable. Shame keeps us small, resentful and afraid.

In an environment where parents, leaders and managers consciously or unconsciously encourage people to connect their self-worth to what they produce or how they behave, the result is disengagement, blame, gossip, stagnation, favouritism and a total dearth of creativity, innovation and joy.

Shame has become embedded in humankind's mind as a belief system about himself. Shame says I am fundamentally wrong, unlovable, worthless, valueless.

To ease that sense of failure—to be accepted and connected with others—we gear our performance accordingly. A part of the experience of shame is the fear of being found out and exposed. We want to run and hide and protect ourselves from exposure to other people's judgment. Sometimes we might even behave badly to create a shaming situation, so we preempt the expectation of judgment we feel others might heap on us for who we are. We 'act up' in self-destructive ways according to the feeling we have about ourselves. This is a very vicious circle.

Many of us start accumulating shame in childhood.

Sometimes the roots of shame involve abuse, neglect, or a significant trauma. But shame can also be rooted in less intense experiences. Shame can be created if a child is told he or she is irresponsible or stupid when he spills his milk, or brings home grades that don't meet a parent's expectations. Rather than being taught how to clean up the spilt milk or helped in ways that might allow for greater success in school, a kind of character assassination takes place which leaves a child believing terrible things about him or herself.

Shame can also be formed when a child's basic need for love and belonging are chronically unmet. When our longing for connection is not met, the basic human need to love and be loved can feel shameful to us.

Unfortunately, accumulated shame does not just go away as time passes. Unless it is addressed directly, we carry shame with us. Sometimes it may seem dormant, but in times of stress, our shame can float to the surface and complicate things—as described above.

For example, a diagnosis of a serious illness can be a trigger for feelings of shame. Being told 'something is seriously wrong with you' can feel very much like the old shaming message of 'you are defective' or 'you can't do anything right.' And when a serious diagnosis becomes public information, we can feel very vulnerable and exposed. As a result, it can be difficult to separate our responses to the current crisis from our responses to old, accumulated shame.

When we experience shame we feel disconnected and desperate for worthiness. Shame can induce self-destructive behaviour(s) and cause us to attack or shame others.

In fact, shame is related to violence, aggression, depression, addiction, self-harm, eating disorders and bullying. Shame cries out for attention, then shuns the very attention it craves.

An example that comes to mind in relationships is where a female spouse might say to a husband or partner, 'I wish you would express your love by touching me more' (thereby expressing a 'love language' that is important to her, but which he is unaware of). What happens next, of course, is that he begins doing just that. His spouse then pulls away and says, 'Don't do it just because I told you to!' The poor guy doesn't know what to do! And this works both ways.

Shame seizes worthiness, or a sense of value elevation, at the expense of trampling on someone else—causing them pain and hurt.

Shame is totally corrosive. It translates every observation into a value statement. When I see no value in myself, I receive observations about my behaviour as value statements.

Shame cannot distinguish between a value statement and an observation

For example, if my wife reminds me to separate the non-recycling and recycling, and I'm suffering with shame, I will receive her reminder not as an observation about my previous failure in this department but as a *negative value statement about me*—that I am useless, careless, stupid, and so forth.

When suffering from shame, I will also compensate by converting any positive observation about my behaviour to an indication that I am, in fact, better than others. I become fixated on judgments about myself in a way that disrupts my relationships with those around me. I constantly need external positive affirmation and become 'high maintenance' (exhausting and demanding) within my relationships.

This is ironic because shame is the fear of disconnection. As human beings, we are psychologically, emotionally, cognitively, and spiritually hard-wired for connection, for love and belonging.

'Shame is the fear that something I have done or failed to do, an ideal I've not lived up to, or a goal that I've not accomplished will make me unworthy of connection.'

Shame has become embedded in Man's mind and belief system about himself. We think we are fundamentally wrong. We think 'I am unlovable and worthless'.

Therefore, if all mankind has this innate need to experience worthiness, love and belonging, it is easy to understand why shame is often described as the 'master emotion.'

Brené Brown[1] the internationally renowned sociologist and self proclaimed 'shame researcher,' decisively cuts open this shame issue, exposes it for what it is and explains the damage it causes. She also suggests ways of becoming *shame-resilient* so that we can begin to live happier, more wholehearted lives. Her books on the subject are well worth studying. Nevertheless, I cannot get away from the fact that all self-help in this area requires a huge amount of self-discipline and self-belief, fuelled by an 'I can defeat shame' attitude. This is not something a lot of people will find easy. It takes courage.

Another mechanism in helping ourselves resist the damaging influence of shame is the importance of verbalising and naming the shame we feel.

Shame hates it when we reach out and tell our story. It hates having words wrapped around it—it cannot survive being unmasked. Shame loves secrecy.

This important aspect of shame-resilience is at its most effective when I am able to share with someone who loves me, someone to whom I am willing to 'bare my soul' and allow to see my imperfections, someone who is truly compassionate.

This is the tricky part. We cannot call on just anyone. A compassionate person is one who has experienced the same darkness as you, and who can be present in your darkness. A compassionate person recognises our shared humanity.

This darkness is a place we all want to run away from. The problem is we take ourselves with us—there is no escape from ourselves that we can manufacture. However, to have some kind of pleasurable existence in life, we learn to manage ourselves. In managing shame, we have two choices, we can let the circumstances of our lives harden us and make us increasingly resentful and afraid, or we can let circumstances soften us and make us kinder.

This choice we have pivots on two factors: either we run and hide from the shame we feel due to the fear of disconnection by building barriers; or we face up to shame and learn to give these feelings space and time, coming to terms with them, recognising that we are not alone in this.

All people experience this shame, this fear—but it need not rule us. *The embracing of this fear will necessitate a dissection of what we actually fear.* It may well entail a 'thinking down to the bottom boards of life'—a place of deep darkness where not many people dare descend.

It may entail you standing still for a while on that stage of life under the spotlight, not knowing who you are, where you are going or where you come from, facing up to these thoughts rather than running away all the time.

In my view, a person who has learnt to wisely manage the darkness of their soul is one who in the midst of the horror of facing the fear of being unlovable, unworthy and isolated, is able not to be too hard on themselves; has learned to love themselves to some degree, and is therefore managing the fear of what others may think about them.

Fortunately, many people find the courage to be vulnerable, to allow the thought to lodge in their minds that someone else sees them as valuable, lovable and worthy, thus making a connection and initiating such an experience of feeling loved and belonging.

❦   4   ❦

LOVE, BELONGING AND CONNECTION

At a natural level, an experience of connection—love and belonging—can be found between good friends whose relationship could be described as one of mutual love. However, there is also the more all-encompassing experience of this sense of love, which is often described as 'falling in love' or 'being in love.' It is possible to love someone, but 'to be in love' is a very different level of experience.

The ancient Greek language has four words for our one English word 'love': *phileo, storge, eros* and *agape*. They describe the following types of love relationships: *phileo*, friendship; *storge*, love for family and children; *eros*, erotic and sensual love; and *agape*—being in love.

Feeling love for someone is a product of what we believe about them, just as hate is the opposite feeling.

This feeling of 'love' may arise purely because of what we (sometimes consciously want to) believe about someone, and it might not be reciprocated.

However, falling in love or being in love necessitates a reciprocal response of belief. What I believe about someone and what they believe about me is the crucial factor—not to mention the chemical, biological factor of attraction! But it is important to point out that the physical attraction two people may feel does not necessarily lead to 'falling in love' or 'being in love'. It may well merely fall into the category of erotic or sensual love.

Needless to say, as humans, we can easily get these 'love' emotions mixed up, and it is a delicate path to tread when we try to explore these things more intently.

I should point out, however, that this natural falling in love may well fulfil the need for love and belonging we are designed for. But there are forces arrayed against such relationships from within and without, and it is possible that either adult in a relationship will begin to feel that the love and belonging they initially felt and expected to continue to receive, does not come up to their expectations. This may lead them to start looking elsewhere.

As we might expect, such a suspicion of failure in expectation quickly leads to a rupture in intimacy. For both parties the tendrils of guilt, followed by shame of failure or rejection, begin rising from the depths of the soul, enveloping the mind *again* with the now strengthened thought, 'I am not good enough, I am a failure.'

Shame is the spectre that haunts the darkness in which all mankind lives. Shame invades the soul, infecting the mind with the thought, 'I am not good enough.'

5

FALLING IN LOVE WITH LOVE

Thinking back on my own life experience, I was a melancholy teenager. I used to enjoy walking alone along the beach considering the great issues of life— why am I here, where am I going and what do I want to do?

Eventually I decided I did not want to continue doing what I realised was pleasing my parents—namely regularly attending the local Anglican Church where I was an altar boy. So, choosing to run off to sea, I left every vestige of religion, along with my Boy Scout uniform, on the doorstep and left home at the age of 17.

At sea I grew up quickly in a male-dominated environment aboard various merchant vessels, sailing the seven seas, visiting major shipping ports around the globe, with all the opportunities these environments provided. However, I fondly remember the nights I spent alone, keeping watch on the bridge in the tropical regions. Under the canopy of an amazing array of stars, and wrapped in warm sultry air, I allowed my thoughts to stray again to the meaning of life, to all those questions I had had as a teenager. On board ship I saw firsthand how men dealt with life when off duty, away from any female companionship for many months. It was not a pretty sight and I did not want to end up like them. But how could I avoid it?

As I progressed professionally it was necessary to attend the University of London for further studies and exams. I stayed in a seedy hotel on the Commercial Road in the east end of London. In those days it was a run-down area due to the recent closing of the India docks. One night in another one of my desperate states of overwhelming loneliness, plagued by increasing thoughts of failure, not only in my exams but also as a person, I cried out, 'God, if you're there, I want to know.'

At that point I opened a Gideon Bible, left in the room by that charity, and started reading. I have no idea where I read but the words started flowing off the page and entering into me, enveloping me in a most indescribable warmth and joy such that I didn't move—indeed, I couldn't move—until I had to leave to attend classes in the morning. I had a smile across my face so wide that after a week or so it really began to hurt! The guys who I was studying with knew something had happened to me, and put it down to some female I had met and fallen for! The rest is history. I somehow connected with a Christian house church group and began a journey of finding out what had happened to me.

From that moment I knew I was totally embraced, included and loved. Shame no longer had a place. However, I would not have used that particular terminology at the time nor during my subsequent journey as a Christian, which included formal theological studies and pastoral training. The emphasis was always more on what I believed about God and what I thought He expected of me, rather than focusing on what He believed to be true about me. In other words, the sneaking strategy of darkness to divert my attention from what God believed about me had an effect and I found myself with an increasing feeling of being inwardly unfulfilled.

The words 'I am not good enough,' occasionally began to trickle into my mind. This unease within began to manifest with the thought that I had to do something for God, get more faith, push in, push up, push through, rather than walk with Him, seeing what He was doing and doing it with Him.

As I look back now, my journey through life has been truly of Him. Nevertheless, there was the increasingly nagging thought that there must be more. That maybe there was something I had lost, an intimacy that was still elusive, a connection that had yet to be made.

I remember reading a book many years before by a writer called E.W. Kenyon. It talked about *who we are 'in Christ.'* He listed all the scriptures which endorsed this perspective. I remember having a very fleeting thought along the lines of 'Huh! That's not you! What a waste of time—who do you think you are?' as I read the book, then rejecting the book entirely and carrying on as I was. I realise now what the book was all about—*what God believed to be true about me.* I no longer had the book, but began to research relevant scriptures and landed on Galatians 2:20 which I chose as my main meditation for that season.

'I have been crucified with Christ. It is no longer I who live, but Christ lives in me and the life that I now live in this body, I live by the faith of the Son of God who loved me and gave Himself for me.'

Then, after quite a long period of meditation on this scripture, a thunderous thought hit me like a train!

'I WAS ALREADY DEAD'.

The statement that Christ died for me two thousand years ago was no longer riddled with distance and delay, cloaked in some mystical concept that failed to have any impact on me, living in the second millennium.

When Christ died, I died. When He rose, I rose. When He sat on His throne, I sat on His lap. I was there on the cross with Him—stretched out across His bosom. When He rose from the dead, I rose with Him.

I saw my stinking flesh distorted in an evil scream of utter anguish and despair, torment and fear, nailed to the cross. My arms of that stinking flesh were pulling at the nails in an attempt to extricate themselves so they could reach out and pull me back into their filthy, slimy grasp, but they could not. I was free at last.

My earthly body is now a mere corpse—as far as darkness is concerned. Satan (the epitome of this present darkness) with all his lies that I am not good enough, and his temptations to try and do better, can come kicking me as much as he likes, but I will not— indeed, I cannot—respond!

If Shame comes knocking at my door, I treat it with the contempt it deserves, like Jesus who *despised the shame*. (see Hebrews 12:2)

From birth Jesus was 'loyal' to His Father. He said, 'No servant can serve two masters, for either he will hate the one and love the other, or else he will be loyal to the one and despise the other' (see Luke 16:13).

All sense of shame has been eradicated. I AM ENOUGH. *I am utterly persuaded about what God believes to be true about me.* I am in love with the Source of Love.

Galatians 2:20 took on new relevance, and I read it this way:

'*...I live by the same faith that Jesus lived by while on this earth—in this darkness—that is, **(he lived by) what God believed to be true about him**'* (Author's additional words and highlighting).

Paul the apostle emphasised the monumental importance of this statement later in his letter to the Galatians, when he said:

'*... the cross of our Lord Jesus Christ, by whom the world is crucified unto me, and I unto the world.*' (Galatians 6:14)

The word 'world' here is the Greek word '*kosmos,*' which refers to the 'government of this world'—namely, the darkness wielding the sword of fear and threat; a weapon that constitutes the root of shame.

This revelation for Paul, and the violent connection with the cross, expresses the absolute radical turn around—'*metanoia*' that affected the way he thought, and subsequently his lifestyle. This identification with the crucifixion is as much a change from death to life, as Adam and Eve experienced in the reverse.

Again, here in his letter to his friend Timothy, Paul was equally persuaded:

The confidence of my calling enables me to overcome every difficulty without shame, for I have an intimate revelation of this God. And my faith in him convinces me that he is more than able to keep all that I've placed in his hands safe and secure until the fullness of his appearing. (2 Timothy 1:12 The Passion Translation).

Paul uses a crucial combination of words here. 'I am not ashamed (anymore!) for I know whom I have believed and I am persuaded...'. Paul was persuaded about what God believed to be true about him. In that case, '*God*', Paul goes on, '*is well able to guard and protect me each day, in whom* (or *in whose word to me*) *I trust.*'

Jesus and Paul knew what the Father believed about them, and lived FROM that belief. We can do that too.

In my book 'What God Believes About You,'[1] I expand on the faith OF the Son of God, in contrast to believing IN God. There is a difference between faith and belief.

What is the opposite to shame? Innocence. Jesus is an example of a man of total innocence.

Innocence is a conscience free from all shame

'As it is written, Behold I am laying in Zion a Stone that will make men stumble, a Rock that will make them fall, but he who believes in Him shall not be put to shame nor be disappointed in his expectations' (Isaiah 28:16 AMP).

God placed His testimony of man's true identity in front of their eyes, in Zion—the centre of their religious focus, yet blinded by their own efforts to justify themselves, they tripped over him. But those who recognise Him as the prototype of their design are freed from the shame of their sense of failure and inferiority.

God has brought the heavenly gavel down on the block decisively; He has made His judgment, and declared you innocent.

6

THE SOUL OF MAN SHAPES HISTORY

I now know that 'shame management', although helpful as a starter, is what it is, merely management. It can never eradicate shame. Shame is the endemic corrosion of the human soul, which is the result of the choice that our forefather Adam made. One of the Bible's unique characteristics is that it forms a record of how human history deals with the soul of man, traced through a specific group of people, and it demonstrates how history has been shaped by and from the attitude of man's soul, manifesting through attitudes of mind, words and actions.

This history of the soul was radically challenged with the coming of Jesus. A new group of people were to emerge with souls impregnated with Love rather than Shame.

Jesus came to reveal humankind as God intended it to be from the beginning, before time began. The incarnated Jesus was the thought the Trinity had about the design of a being called 'Adām'—Mankind.

This is the main reason Jesus is referred to as the last Adam; *'The first Adām was made a living soul, the last Adām was made a quickening spirit'* (1 Corinthians 15:45). The word 'quickening' has been translated from two Greek words meaning 'life' and 'to make.'

Therefore, you could say the last Adam was 'a living breathing being.' (The word for 'spirit' is pneuma—wind or breath). So, we have, 'The first Adām was made a living soul, the last Adām a living breathing being.'

This makes sense. There is no difference! Jesus is a manifestation of the first Adām or Man. They are of the same design. Jesus is 'the rock' out of which Adām was hewn. That is, Adām as he would have been had he remained in the garden, intimate with his Lord. Paul is clear about this when he wrote to the people of the city of Philippi about Jesus taking on human form, in chapter 2, verses 5-7: 'Have the same mindset as Christ Jesus: Who, being in very nature God, did not consider equality with God something to be used to his own advantage;

rather, he made himself nothing by taking the very nature of a servant, being made in human likeness'.

Jesus comes to introduce us to the context of eternity, an eternity of being connected to the Trinity, fully accepted and loved. In this context, all the temporal stuff loses its importance. In God, before time began, there was no career, education, language, race, or any of those other things upon which we often hang our identity. Jesus introduces you to a context in which every temporal reference you could refer to, or find yourself in, disappears!

We have allowed our shame, achievements, disappointment, careers, culture, and so on to define us. God has a different definition, an eternal definition. He says that you are his image and likeness and that not even a fraction of who you are has been revealed yet! That's why he is eager to unveil this mystery to us—and to go on unveiling it, and unveiling it for eternity!

✣   7   ✣

YOU HAVE DIED TO SHAME

'For the love of Christ constrains us having concluded this, that since one died for all, therefore all died' (2 Corinthians 5:14).

In this statement Paul the apostle makes a crucial observation. That it was not just ONE man that died on the cross, but Christ embraced the whole of humanity, past, present and future in himself. It was this realisation that caused pandemonium in Satan's HQ! The first letter Paul wrote to the people of Corinth (Chapter 2:8) makes this plain... *'None of the princes of this world knew: for had they known it, they would not have crucified the Lord of glory.'*

The crucifixion marked the total and final defeat of the hold darkness had over mankind. The hold that Shame, that silent killer, had had over all mankind was finally broken. The word 'sin' is usually the word used in this context, but the word 'shame' is a better interpretation.

Sin and Shame

Shame and sin are the same thing, more or less—shame being the consequence of sin. Jesus defined sin thus: 'The world's sin is unbelief in me' (John 16:9).

Jesus linked sin to unbelief. This statement has often been used to refer to people who do not 'believe in Jesus' as sinners. But I often ask the question; what does 'not believing in Jesus' actually *mean?*'

In the light of what we have discussed so far, not believing in Jesus is not believing what he believes to be true about me—that I am good enough, I am worthy, I am loved, I do belong.

Sin therefore is linked to shame because it believes 'I am not good enough, I am a failure,' and shame is the outworking of this belief. Therefore, the 'sins' we commit are the resultant behaviour of what we believe about ourselves. *In other words, sin is the lifestyle that results when you continue to believe a lie about yourself.*

How can I experience this falling in love with Love?

Thinking about this question has occupied my thoughts for some time, because like Paul, '*I labour until Christ be formed in all of you*' (Galatians 4:19).

I long for all people to experience this fullness available to them '*in Christ*'. But Jesus 'knew from the beginning who the sceptics were and who his traitor would be'. He had warned his followers, '*There are still some of you who will not believe*'. In spite of everything He had done and been! He went on to make the sobering statement: '*No one embraces me unless the Father has given you to me*' (John 6:65).

So, is it ONLY our Father God who initiates any experience of an intimate relationship between us and Jesus? Is there nothing I can do?

Let's imagine such an experience of love happening to a girl in a natural sense. How does she 'fall in love'? Generally, it is the boy who traditionally initiates a relationship with a girl. Boy likes girl—opens up conversation, dating begins and he cherishes her with his words and actions. He believes things about her that she could not imagine about herself. Eventually she begins to believe what he believes to be true about her, rather than what she believes about herself (which to some degree has its roots in shame).

She believes things about him too, that he may not have believed about himself, so the experience of love develops in this fertile ground of what one believes about the other. These thoughts begin to override their own beliefs about themselves. The connection is made, love and belonging is discovered, and this becomes the foundation of any future relationship.

Why should there be any difference in how the Father draws us to Himself through Jesus? After all, He is the Source—Love Himself—and there is no gender in Love.

If I cannot initiate this experience of love, is there anything I can do to allow this initiation to begin, or to become more real to me? Yes, I think there is, through taking seriously His thoughts about me – being willing to consider what He believes about me must be true!

As I've already described, I did this using those verses in Galatians 2:20 as a starting point. The rest is up to the Holy Spirit, who makes the links. The way that happens is the exciting aspect of being cherished. No-one else will speak such words of love, value and worth over you, so you have to listen to the Father speaking it, and repeat it over yourself until you fully believe it. The apostle Paul describes this process as 'renewing your mind. '...*so that you may <u>prove</u>* (that is, recognise as genuine after examination, to approve, deem worthy, even experience) *that you are included, loved and worthy'* (Romans 12:2 Mirror Bible).

The words of this song, '*And the moment I can feel that you feel that way too, is when I fall in love with you*', express it well—feelings follow thoughts.

So, change how and what you think about yourself by thinking what He thinks about you, and the feelings will follow. To do this you need to read what He says about you in the bible! You have a helper; God's Holy Spirit is always working to bring this intimate connection to completion—it is His joy!

When you first start focusing and meditating on these scriptures there is pressure to give up, because they seem to rattle around in the mind without any real substance. But persevere. The author of the book of Hebrews, in chapter 4:11 describes this as the only labour we need to engage in, 'labour to enter into the rest,' he says, 'lest any man fall after the same example of unbelief' (The writer is warning you not to fail to believe what God believes about you!)

8

A NOTE ABOUT DARKNESS

Luke quotes in the New Testament from the Old Testament book written by Isaiah:

'The people who sat in darkness have seen a great light, and upon those who sat in the region and shadow of death, Light has dawned' (Matthew 4:16, with a parallel in Luke 1:79).

John, one of the disciples, writes what Jesus said about Himself with regard to the darkness:

'I have come as light into the world, that whoever believes in me should not abide in darkness' (John 12:46).

The darkness, the lie under which the world labours, is how Jesus also describes the condition of all mankind in the verse above, the lie having been around from the beginning; essentially, the words of Satan (Genesis 3) conveying that if you do this or that thing, you can become like God.

Our enemy's damning implication was this: You are not like God—you are not enough(!) but you can become like Him, become what you were originally created to be, find your place, become someone of value and worth—if you DO something.

Adām's acceptance of that lie was confirmed by the taking and eating of the fruit. It is significant that the scriptures describe Adām and Eve as *not ashamed*, although they were naked, <u>before</u> they ate the fruit (Genesis 2:25).

<u>After</u> eating Satan's bait Adam and Eve's nakedness became something they had to cover up. Have you ever wondered why?

I submit that the intimacy they experienced prior to this event, although they did not recognise it as intimacy, was lost. Suddenly they were self-conscious before one another and before God, exposed in a way they had not experienced before. The temptation of suspicion (suspicion that God was holding out on them, that He did not accept them unless they made themselves acceptable), upon which they acted, is the enemy of intimacy.

Shame entered in, with that overwhelming sense of failure which has plagued mankind ever since. We want to run and hide; protect ourselves from exposure to one another's judgment and from God's—so we think. We have been doing this ever since.

It has been said that very few people are prepared to think 'down to the bottom boards' of life. If they do, they are in danger of going mad, becoming super-religious or committing suicide. For many, the only way out of such a dark place seems to be the latter.

I submit that the darkness that mankind lives in now, this side of physical death, continues after physical death as well. That the only way out is through the Death that all mankind has already been included in— the Death of Christ. This is the most important death, as far as God is concerned.

Physical death is merely a transition from one realm of darkness to another, much more acute and isolated, darkness. But just as the gospel is available this side of physical death so it will be still available in the darkness on the other side.

'He rescued us from the power of darkness and brought us safe into the kingdom of his dear Son' (Colossians 1:13).

9

THE HIDDEN REEF IN OUR INTIMACY

As I said earlier, Shame entered into our human ancestors as an overwhelming sense of failure which has plagued mankind ever since, being the hidden reef in all our intimate encounters.

Shame has a mercurial character and hates being exposed. It is the source of vile accusations that are flung at us when we even begin to dig down through our soul to ask the question, 'Why am I the way I am?.' And very few people have the courage or fortitude even to do this. There have been a multitude of 'self-help' books written over the years which seek to give people a measure of emotional stability in an unstable, fickle world.

But the most important words that will unshackle us from our plight are the words that are found, as far as most people think, within the best-selling book that remains the least read (certainly the least studied)—the Bible.

To read the gospels and soak in the words of Jesus; to pick up on the intention behind his actions and to meditate on the few stories in which those suffering from shame encountered Him (the alienated woman at the well; the wife caught in adultery; the gatecrasher and prostitute who covered him in expensive perfume; the greedy taxman who climbed a tree to catch a glimpse of him, or the good friend who betrayed him). These humans experienced, in their brief encounters with Him, an eradication of shame few of us can understand.

The Mind as a Garden

Imagine your mind as a garden, a wild unkept forgotten garden. If left to their own devices, the brambles and weeds will grow into an interlocking canopy of frightful proportions. Just looking at and considering how to tackle such a tangle is overwhelming!

However, as many of you have probably experienced, once you get on your hands and knees and break through the initial wall of thorns, you discover that this tangled canopy is only supported by scattered clumps of roots, certainly not as many as you anticipated! Once you start chopping the foliage at the root, it all pulls away easily in large swathes.

Your shame produces a large foreboding canopy of thorns and thistles to trap you in its grip, while all the time the stems of these brambles grow out from a few clumps! Get your secateurs out and start cutting away today. Use the truth of what God believes about you to cut away the untruths. You will find that the work is not that hard, the Holy Spirit just loves gardening, and will come alongside you to help!

I would like to refer you to my book, 'What God Believes About You' for a list of helpful scriptures and comments to use as tools in your gardening endeavours.

This 'work' of meditation is the only 'work' that we can contribute to the process of having our minds transformed. The New Testament tells us that it is God's work actually, in the letter to the Roman underground church, 'Do not conform to the pattern of this world, but be transformed by the renewing of your mind' (Romans 12:2). We just have to let him do it.

When the disciples asked Jesus, '...*what shall we do, that we may work the works of God?*', *Jesus answered and said to them, 'This is the work of God, that **you believe in Him whom He sent**' (John 6:28-29 NKJV).*

So, we come full circle—back to the Master who 'despised the shame,' back to being persuaded and believing what God, as Jesus, believes about you!

CONCLUSION

Practical Steps

There are five emotions that are supported by the root of shame. Like a canopy over our soul and mind they seriously hinder the experience of freedom from being at peace with ourselves, which we earnestly desire. Anger, hatred, anxiety, grief and fear, at different times and with different intensities, spiral around our being like the tentacles of an octopus whose dark intentions keep us imprisoned.

If we were able stand aside from ourselves and look at ourselves dispassionately, we might understand we are all part of a material sociocultural dynamic that our particular cultural upbringing has programmed us with, where winning—being successful—is the correlative of material entitlement. It does not take long to realise that losing is not an option. Our highly competitive socialisation may work well for some. For others it only seems to impose shame for what are natural inadequacies, and guilt for what are believed to be sins and failures. A person may have meritorious intent, but over the years I've witnessed the profoundly disabling effects of such malevolent programming. Indeed, I have suffered from it myself. When you are 'in it' it is very difficult to get out of it. The degrees of darkness that shrouds our thinking, and any determination we may summon up to 'do something about it,' can rise up and swamp us, whispering, 'What if this doesn't work?' 'It will never work,' 'You are not good enough to deserve that' etc. The voice of shame attacks our self-worth by questioning our ability, performance and identity. It is very easy to become saturated with discouragement, and simply give up.

Discouraged people become angry and internalise their anger by engaging in subconscious self-destruction. Hatred is fermented anger, and it can destroy nations, as history demonstrates. Imagine, then, what it does to you.

We are all capable of taking control of our minds, but the unconscious battering of the indoctrination to believe we are undeserving has taken its toll. Not everyone can be a winner, and chronic loss often leads to increased feelings of failure, guilt, and shame. Initially many people may have been angry and bitter at the world for depriving them, but eventually that anger and bitterness become internalised.

After a life of losing, the prospect of losing life seems a fitting end. When blaming others for my predicament— my failure—loses its tenuous legitimacy, the next option is God. He has always been the best and final option.

If you were to ask yourself honestly, 'How deserving of a life of abundant health, love, and happiness do I feel I am?' on a scale of 'one to ten', with ten being the highest, what number would you settle on?

This little exercise often sparks introspection, and further in-depth conversation. Many are all too willing to discuss their **binds** to guilt, shame, and anger. Failure and inadequacy are normal facts of life, but far too many of us have become inwardly enraged from the resultant self-contempt. Failure, guilt, and shame fan the flames of anger, blocking any light of love, validation, worth and acceptance that is genuinely offered. The passionate power of love towards you totally envelops your very being, which 'stands on tiptoe' in desperate hope for an invitation to flood in and begin to repair all the damage and wounds, is sadly often seen as the very source of our unworthiness and un-deservedness, and is therefore rejected.

Opening the Door to Freedom

I recommend a three step process to opening the door to a wholeness and a deep joy that will fulfil you.

1. The door handle. The intentional act of gripping the door handle is the first step to opening the door, as you invite in the overwhelming power of love and total acceptance. The door handle represents being gentle with yourself, being kind towards yourself.

2. Push down on the door handle by forgiving yourself. The pressure of self-forgiveness is easier to apply as you visualise yourself being enveloped in a multidimensional kaleidoscope of colour, light, love, well-being, acceptance and value. This root of shame—this darkness, this faceless octopus with its slimy tentacles is no more than an infinitesimally small back spot in this huge dimension, easily extinguished by opening the door.

3. The next step is the open the door. Invite in the author—the Wisdom and power that uphold this universal, multidimensional wholeness of joy, peace, love and acceptance. Let the King of Wisdom enfold your whole being, imagine yourself being entwined

within the strands of beautiful life and wholeness. Separation is an illusion. That place of darkness through which you saw yourself is nothing more than a kind of potion designed to keep us all in a state of 'suspended animation'. Like in the story of sleeping beauty, we are all waiting for the kiss of love to awaken us! The God of absolute love, Mr Love Himself is a resplendent energy that resides within and all around us.

Neuroscientists are now saying that happiness is a learned skill and that, by re-training our thoughts, we can map out new nerve pathways that reshape the joy connections in our brain. They also tell us that repetition is important. By continually rehearsing positive thoughts and perceptions, we give direction to our reality architects—the mind and brain—to construct a domain of unconditional joy. True heartfelt joy doesn't come naturally to most of those who've been raised in this highly conditional culture, but it can be realised through grace and dedication to spiritual cultivation.

What Next?

After opening the door, I hear you ask 'What next?' Further spiritual cultivation sounds like work, it sounds like we have to get our trowels and start digging up the roots of shame. In fact there is a 'doing without doing'. This higher wisdom, which is available to all, suggests there is abundant joy awaiting the seeker who allows it to come to their attention. Scripture, and the New Testament in particular, reminds us that within the silent depths of our immortal inner heart there is a wellspring of joy. Then when we close our eyes, empty our hands, and silence our noise we will at last see, touch, and hear all the true joy that has forever awaited us.

NOTES

1. SHAME: ENEMY OF WHOLEHEARTED LIVING

1. https://www.psychologytoday.com/us/blog/your-zesty-self/200905/what-we-get-wrong-about-shame

3. PERFORMANCE SHAME

1. Brown, Brené. Daring Greatly. How the Courage to Be Vulnerable Transforms the Way We Live, Love, Parent and Lead. Penguin. 2012

5. FALLING IN LOVE WITH LOVE

1. Wilks, Peter. 'What God believes About You.' Onwards and Upwards. 2019. Available from www.1thing.life or Amazon.co.uk

What God Believes About You.

The book title is inspired by C.S Lewis, who made the statement:

'What God believes about you is more important than what you believe about God'.

This perspective radically changes the way we see ourselves, and the way we read and understand scripture. The book seeks to highlight how God actually sees you as INCLUDED in the Trinity, from whom you have never been excluded.

It also uncovers the mis-information that has been presented over the concept of hell since the 5th Century.

It promotes the ideas that heaven and hell are both 'states of being' rather than places we go to when we die; and that physical death has no bearing on where we spend eternity.

It argues that the death which actually does have an impact on our state of being—either side of physical death—is the death we all died 'in Christ.' The book posits that, for those who die physically without having believed this truth, the gospel is still available to them.

Available on Amazon.co.uk or www.1thing.life

For further information on all publications and other topics please go to the author's website: www.1thing.life

www.ingramcontent.com/pod-product-compliance
Lightning Source LLC
Chambersburg PA
CBHW051007050726
47592CB00007B/2749